D1443677

Benedict Arnold

Traitor to the Cause

Colonial Leaders

Lord Baltimore *English Politician and Colonist*

Benjamin Banneker *American Mathematician and Astronomer*

William Bradford *Governor of Plymouth Colony*

Benjamin Franklin *American Statesman, Scientist, and Writer*

Anne Hutchinson *Religious Leader*

Cotton Mather *Author, Clergyman, and Scholar*

William Penn *Founder of Democracy*

John Smith *English Explorer and Colonist*

Miles Standish *Plymouth Colony Leader*

Peter Stuyvesant *Dutch Military Leader*

Revolutionary War Leaders

Benedict Arnold *Traitor to the Cause*

Nathan Hale *Revolutionary Hero*

Alexander Hamilton *First U.S. Secretary of the Treasury*

Patrick Henry *American Statesman and Speaker*

Thomas Jefferson *Author of the Declaration of Independence*

John Paul Jones *Father of the U.S. Navy*

Thomas Paine *Political Writer*

Paul Revere *American Patriot*

Betsy Ross *American Patriot*

George Washington *First U.S. President*

Benedict Arnold

Traitor to the Cause

Norma Jean Lutz

Arthur M. Schlesinger, jr.
Senior Consulting Editor

Chelsea House Publishers

Philadelphia

Dedication: To Bennett and Sherry—a neat set of parents.

Produced by 21st Century Publishing and Communications, Inc. New York, NY. http://www.21cpc.com

CHELSEA HOUSE PUBLISHERS
Editor in Chief Stephen Reginald
Production Manager Pamela Loos
Director of Photography Judy L. Hasday
Art Director Sara Davis
Managing Editor James D. Gallagher

Staff for *BENEDICT ARNOLD*
Project Editor/Publishing Coordinator Jim McAvoy
Associate Art Director Takeshi Takahashi
Series Design Keith Trego

The Chelsea House World Wide Web address is
http://www.chelseahouse.com

3 5 7 9 8 6 4 2

Library of Congress Cataloging-in-Publication Data

Lutz, Norma Jean.
Benedict Arnold / by Norma Jean Lutz.
80 pp. cm. — (Revolutionary War Leaders series)
Includes bibliographical references and index.
Summary: A biography of the infamous traitor who sold secret military information to the British army during the American Revolution.
ISBN 0-7910-5358-X (hc)   ISBN 0-7910-5701-1 (pb)
1. Arnold, Benedict, 1741-1801—Juvenile literature. 2. American loyalists—United States—Biography—Juvenile literature. 3. Generals—United States—Biography—Juvenile literature. 4. United States—Continental Army—Biography—Juvenile literature. 5. United States—History—Revolution, 1775-1783—Biography—Juvenile literature. [1. Arnold, Benedict, 1741-1801. 2. American loyalists. 3. Generals. 4. United States—History—Revolution, 1775-1783—Biography.] I. Title. II. Series.
E278.A7L87   1999
973.3'82'092—dc21   99-20422
[B]   CIP

Publisher's Note: In Colonial and Revolutionary War America, there were no standard rules for spelling, punctuation, capitalization, or grammar. Some of the quotations that appear in the Colonial Leaders and Revolutionary War Leaders series come from original documents and letters written during this time in history. Original quotations reflect writing inconsistencies of the period.

Contents

Students in class at a colonial school. As a schoolboy, Benedict covered up the fact that he was a coward by acting loud, conceited, and temperamental.

A Headstrong Boy

In the small town of Norwich, Connecticut, there lived a daredevil of a boy who was often the talk of the town. His name was Benedict Arnold. Benedict's wild tricks caused the residents of Norwich to shake their heads in wonder. Born January 14, 1741, Benedict's earliest years were lived in comfort. His father made many different wooden containers and was a successful **cooper**. The family's wealth allowed them to sit in the front pews at church that were saved for the "first" families of the community. The family also made enough money to send young Benedict to a fine private school in Canterbury, Connecticut.

At school Benedict was known for his loud voice, quick temper, and conceited manner. His teachers tried to help him to correct these character flaws, but had no success. Later Benedict would admit that he was also a coward during these years, a problem he would battle head-on for years.

Meanwhile, things were not going well at home. During an outbreak of yellow fever, two of Benedict's sisters died. Only his sister Hannah was left. Benedict's father, who had begun to live as if he were richer than he really was, was now facing business failure. Mr. Arnold had borrowed money for years, but with the business not doing well, he was now unable to repay his debts. The creditors were pressing him for the money and he could not settle his outstanding accounts.

When Benedict turned 14 the family business finally collapsed and he was brought home from the school. If that wasn't embarrassing enough,

Benedict's father turned to drinking to escape his sadness. Many times, the boy had to go to the local tavern and bring his drunken father home. This opened the way for Benedict to become the butt of the town jokes. In whispers and out loud, the other boys made fun of him. This treatment may have increased Benedict's feelings of cowardice.

At some point, something happened inside Benedict. He made the decision not to be a victim any longer. He began fighting his tormentors, often picking a fight first and always taking on the bigger boys. Driven by sheer determination, he often won. The more he won, the more confident and daring he became. Younger boys followed him to see what stunt he would come up with next. A natural athlete, Benedict could leap over a wagon or crawl up the highest mast of a ship in the harbor. He was also a very good skater.

One day he was with a group of boys at the gristmill where the huge water wheel turned round and round. In a fit of daring, Benedict swam out to the wheel, grabbed one of the slippery arms and rode the wheel around. He was lifted high into the air, brought down and plunged into the water, then lifted high once more. Laughing gaily, he jumped free and swam to safety. The boys asked him to do it again and again. Benedict did so, but he was looking for more daring tricks.

Another time a house in the community caught fire. When all attempts to put out the flames had failed, the townspeople stood by watching helplessly. Suddenly, there appeared a figure up on the ridgepole that ran down the peak of the roof. It was Benedict. His arms were out-stretched like a tightrope walker. With flames leaping around him, he walked the length of the pole and escaped unharmed. The citizens of Norwich shook their heads, wondering what kind of a wild boy this was.

Being the center of attention became very important to Benedict. The more exciting the stunts, the more his cowardice melted away, until he felt he'd conquered his fears forever.

There was a custom in New England to set bonfires on the hillsides every Thanksgiving Eve. An ordinary bonfire wasn't suitable for Benedict. Gathering his friends, he directed them to help carry lumber and kindling to the top of the highest hill. Next they went to a local shipyard and stole barrels of tar. In his imagination, Benedict could see the biggest bonfire in the town's history. Thankfully, the town constable came on the scene. When caught, Benedict put up his fists and threatened to fight the constable. Being a wise man, the officer simply took Benedict home to his mother.

By now, Mrs. Arnold was frantic. What could be done with this headstrong boy? She thought of her cousins, Daniel and Joshua Lathrop, who owned an **apothecary** store in town. She decided to **apprentice** Benedict to her cousins. Perhaps learning a trade would help to settle the boy down.

The Lathrops were known far and wide for their fine selections of healing herbs and ointments. Other products such as fine wines and imported silks were also sold at the store. The Lathrops lived in a lovely mansion furnished with finery from London. Their stables were full of beautiful horses, and slaves catered to their needs. Living with the Lathrops reminded Benedict how much he had lost when his father's business failed. He remembered how important wealth could be, and how nice it felt to be dressed in stylish clothes and to have people respect him.

As much as Benedict liked money and fine things, he also loved adventure. More than anything he wanted to go to war and be a hero. At this time the British were fighting with the French, and he wanted to help beat the French. Protestant New Englanders were taught to hate the French, who were Catholic, so Benedict hated them too.

In the summer of 1757 the French, along

When Benedict was an apprentice, he lived with the Lathrops in a large house like this one. Living an upper-class lifestyle made Benedict want to grow up to become famous and rich.

with their Indian friends, came to within 100 miles of the Massachusetts border. A call went out for all available men to join the local

Ships battle during the French and Indian War. At 16 Benedict joined the militia to fight the French. But he missed a chance to be a hero because his group never saw action.

militia. Even though Benedict was only 16, the Lathrop brothers allowed him to go.

With his musket in hand and dreams of adventure in his head, he marched off to fight.

In less than two weeks, the militia received word that the fighting was over and that the French had taken over Fort William Henry on Lake George. Benedict was not only disappointed but also filled with more hatred for the French. Now he had to return to the routine of sweeping floors and waiting on customers in the apothecary shop. He'd had his first taste of war, but his chance to become a hero would have to wait a while longer.

The busy streets of colonial New Haven, Connecticut. After his father's death, Benedict moved to New Haven to open a store. Although he appeared to be wealthy, Benedict actually went deeply into debt.

In Search
of Adventure

When Benedict's mother died in 1760, his father's drinking increased. Time and again, Benedict came to his father's rescue. Those humiliating experiences caused him to long for respect and dignity. These problems finally came to an end when the elder Arnold died in 1761. The next year, Benedict finished his apprentice period. The Lathrops asked him to stay on, but that would never do for Benedict. There was adventure to be had and it was not in Norwich, Connecticut.

With the 500 pounds of British money given to him by the kindly Lathrop brothers, Benedict went to New Haven to open his own store. His plan was to become very wealthy. The first step was to travel to London to purchase the stock for his new store.

While in London, dressed in the finest clothes, Benedict went on a wild buying spree. His look of success fooled many business owners into offering him credit. He purchased fine books, wines, paints, watches, medicines, clothing for himself, and a beautiful carriage. All told, he spent over 3,000 pounds.

Once back in New Haven, he felt it necessary to keep up the appearance of immense wealth. He rode about town in his carriage and wore the latest London fashions, which included pointy-toed shoes with shiny buckles. His creditors soon learned that money due them was slow in coming. When Benedict was pressed about the debts, he told them "later." He was able to keep up appearances for almost two years. Finally he wound up in debtors' prison for six weeks.

For most people this would have been a

turning point, but not for Benedict. He never changed his way of living or his way of doing business. He decided to turn his attentions to the shipping business, where there was money to be made. He sold the family farm in Norwich to raise money. Since his sister, Hannah, was still living there, he brought her to New Haven and put her in charge of running the store.

Hannah was an obedient sister. At one time she had been in love with a man, but Benedict chased him off. After all, the man was a hated Frenchman! Benedict drew his pistol on the man once and threatened to kill him. The Frenchman never returned. Hannah spent the rest of her life working hard and being a good sister to Benedict.

For the next few years, Captain Benedict Arnold was in control of his own ships, which pleased him greatly. On land he was as cocky as ever, gaining more enemies than friends as he sailed from port to port. Honor was of great importance to Benedict, and he would fight a

**Workers load ships in a bustling harbor.
To make more money and have more
adventures, Benedict eagerly went into
the shipping business.**

duel at the drop of a hat. Not satisfied with simply

trading, he also did a great deal of smuggling of

forbidden articles. This risky business lent an air

of adventure, which Benedict still craved.

Early signs of unrest in the colonies were surfacing at this time. The new British ruler, King George III, seemed fair enough when he first came into power. Later, however, he began imposing unbearable restrictions on the colonies.

In the midst of these upheavals, Benedict fell in love with Margaret (Peggy) Mansfield. He was 26 and Peggy was 22 when they married in 1767. A daughter of the local sheriff, Peggy turned out to be a good wife to Benedict. Three sons were born to them—Benedict Jr., Richard, and Henry.

When Benedict was at sea, he disliked not hearing from his wife. Sometimes Peggy would go for months without writing to him. By 1773 he had had enough of these long separations, and gave up life at sea. Being at home gave him a chance to oversee the building of his magnificent two-story house on Water Street. Benedict was also able to pay attention to the growing conflict between the **Tories** (those in sympathy with Britain) and the **Patriots** (those who were loyal to the American colonists).

In December 1774 a number of New Haven gentlemen gathered to form a militia. The Footguards, as they were called, wore fine uniforms with scarlet coats and silver buttons. On March 15, 1775, Benedict was elected as their captain. He liked the colorful uniforms, the drilling, and the parades. He also liked giving orders. The very next month, when news came that fighting had broken out in Lexington and Concord, Massachusetts, Benedict was eager to join the battle.

Not all the New Haven citizens agreed. They felt it was too dangerous to openly oppose the king. Benedict didn't care about these opinions. He rallied his Footguards and asked the committeemen for the keys to the **powder house**. His request was denied because the townsmen had decided to remain neutral. Benedict, accustomed to getting his own way, said if he did not get the keys, he and his men would break the door down. The townsmen finally gave in and gave him the keys.

As Benedict and his men marched with great

The battle at Concord, Massachusetts, which began the Revolutionary War. Captain Benedict Arnold eagerly led his militia toward the war–and, he hoped, toward fame and glory for himself.

anticipation toward Cambridge, the center for the American resistance, their fine uniforms drew a lot of attention. Most of the other fighters were a ragtag bunch right off the nearby farms.

Along the way, Benedict heard many reports of the serious shortage of guns and ammunition. How could the Americans fight if they had no weapons to fight with?

By the time Benedict reached Cambridge, he had hatched an idea. He went straight to the Committee of Safety in charge of military matters. There he offered to lead an expedition against Fort Ticonderoga, where the British had a number of cannons, guns, and ammunition. While the members of the committee felt that war would come very soon, there as yet had been no actual declaration of war. Taking a fort would be considered an act of **aggression**. The situation was touchy. But in the end the committee decided to give Benedict 10 horses, 100 pounds, permission to raise an army of 400 men, and orders to take Fort Ticonderoga. In addition, Benedict was promoted to the rank of colonel. He was delighted.

During the period before the war, the colonies were not completely united. For decades each colony had acted separately, and sometimes they were at total odds with one another. It would take time for the idea of being united to take hold. As Benedict was gathering men, a captain in Connecticut had enlisted the help of the Green Mountain Boys to do the same job—take Fort Ticonderoga.

The well-known Green Mountain Boys were a wild bunch of mountaineers from an area called the Hampshire Grants (later Vermont). These men were led by a huge fighting man named Ethan Allen. All of them hated "Yorkers," as they called the people from New York. They thought it would be great fun to take a fortress that was located in New York. These wild and woolly men had never even heard of Benedict.

With less than 100 men, Benedict Arnold and
Ethan Allen seized Fort Ticonderoga. Because
the colonists surprised the British, the fort was
taken without a single shot being fired.

A Fearless
Leader

ort Ticonderoga was located at the southern
end of Lake Champlain. The north-south
invasion route between Canada and the colonies
was a waterway formed by Lake Champlain and
Lake George. Both the French and English had
used this natural water route in previous wars.
Both had built forts along it. Fort Ticonderoga was
one of those strategic forts.

When Benedict got word that another group was
planning to take the fort, he hurried ahead with his
valet to find them. He instructed his own men to
round up recruits and follow later. He found the

Green Mountain Boys in a tavern 25 miles from the fort. When he stepped inside, he found a room full of rowdy, boisterous, drinking frontiersmen. Using his most firm commander's voice, Benedict waved his papers from the Committee of Safety and announced he was now their leader. The Green Mountain Boys just laughed.

They informed Benedict that they had a leader and his name was Ethan Allen. At the time of Benedict's arrival, Allen was away at a staging area. When Ethan Allen returned and saw the official papers from Massachusetts, he respected them. But his men threatened to quit and go home if they had to serve under a dandy like Benedict. In the end it was decided the two leaders would enter the fort side by side.

The plan was to take the fort by night, but there were no boats to ferry the men across the river. By the time boats were located, a terrible thunderstorm struck and slowed the transport. As dawn came on May 11th, they decided to take the fort without waiting for the full force.

About 85 men were involved in the attack.

With the element of surprise on their side, they were successful. The British commander came to the door with his "breeches in his hand." Allen ordered that the fort be given over instantly. When the commander asked by what authority, Allen answered, "In the name of the great Jehovah and the Continental Congress." The commander handed over his sword to Ethan Allen, which proved to be a great humiliation to Benedict. Fort Ticonderoga was taken without a shot being fired.

For a short time, Benedict held command of the fort. He supervised every detail and enjoyed every

In July 1775 Ethan Allen was commissioned as an advance scout for a regiment moving into Canada. Allen sent supplies back to his regiment and recruited Canadians along the way. In a reckless move, Allen attempted to take over Montreal with his small band of recruits. Reinforcements failed to show up and Allen's men deserted him. On September 25, 1775, he was captured by the enemy and shipped to Britain in chains. There he narrowly escaped being hanged as a traitor. He spent three years as a prisoner and missed most of the hard fighting.

minute of it. His own men had arrived on May 14, along with an additional 50 recruits. The Green Mountain Boys went home to tend their farms, and Ethan Allen was busy writing letters to get support for a full-scale attack on Canada. For a short time Benedict was happy.

In June, Colonel Hinman from Connecticut came to take over command. With him were 1,000 troops. Benedict was to be second in command. He considered this an outrage. Why had he been allowed to take the fort if he were not going to be allowed to command it? In addition, a committee from Massachusetts investigated Benedict's actions. They asked that he account for his expenses,

---

After a very difficult battle at Breed's Hill, General George Washington saw the need for the cannons from Fort Ticonderoga as a vital necessity to protect the Boston area. Henry Knox, a bookseller from Boston, was made commander of the artillery and assigned to get the big guns. Knox chose 59 of the cannons for a wintry 300-mile trip to Boston. The heavy guns were hauled by sleighs pulled over the snow by teams of yoked oxen. The guns were used to fortify Bunker Hill, helping to repel the British onslaught there.

which were many times over what they had authorized him to spend. Furious at this questioning of his honesty, he resigned on the spot and took his men with him.

When he arrived home, Hannah met him with the terrible news that his wife had died while he was away. Hannah was doing her best to take care of the children and run the business. Saddened and discouraged, Benedict became bedridden for weeks with an attack of gout, a disease causing inflamed joints.

While his body was resting quietly, his mind actively continued to plan. His thoughts were on Canada. Canada had belonged to the British for only 12 years. It was filled with French people who were not totally loyal to the British king. Surely an invasion of Canada would be successful. All the French people would come to the side of the Americans, and Benedict would be the conquering hero.

Later that summer, Benedict finally had the opportunity to meet George Washington in person. (Washington had just been chosen to be the Commander of the Continental Army.) The two liked each other from the first time they met. Washington could see a fearless leader in Benedict. Washington was planning a two-pronged attack on Canada. One regiment would go up Lake Champlain to Montreal; the other would go overland through the wilderness of Maine. Benedict was put in command of the wilderness campaign. The trip, Benedict told Washington, would take about 20 days.

By September, Benedict had his army of over 1,000 men ready to sail from Newburyport, Massachusetts. Some of these riflemen, under the command of Colonel Daniel Morgan, were experienced frontiersmen. Others were not as skilled. They would be traveling through unex-plored country, but no one seemed concerned.

The 200 **bateaux** that Benedict had ordered to carry his men and supplies up the rivers were a cause for great concern. They had been constructed with green lumber and were sure

George Washington liked Benedict and respected him as a brave leader. Washington put Benedict in charge of an important wilderness campaign into Canada.

to leak as the wet wood warped and bent. The carpenter stated that he had never had such a large order and did not have enough properly seasoned wood, so he *had* to use green wood. The boats were patched over, the supplies loaded, and the army set out on its journey.

The men soon learned that the rivers were nearly impossible to navigate. They ran in twisting, turning fashion with more heavy waterfalls and boiling rapids than anyone could have imagined. The river trip had already taken more time than Benedict had allotted for the entire journey. Then the rains came in torrents, ruining much of the supplies and swelling the rivers to their limits. One colonel turned back with his entire division. Although he was branded a coward, his leaving probably saved the expedition since there were fewer men to feed.

By the time the snow began to fall, the men were reduced to boiling the leather from their moccasins and bags to make broth. Two of the pet dogs were killed, "which the distressed soldiers ate with good appetite, even the feet and skins." Near the end of the journey, Benedict went ahead with an advance party to purchase meat and flour for the starving men.

On December 2, 1775, Benedict and his men finally met up with General Montgomery's forces, which had come up to Montreal by boat. The two leaders decided to wait for the cover of a snowstorm to attack the city. The opportunity came on New Year's Eve. Montgomery's men would come from south of the city, and Benedict's men would come by way of Lower Town. But the British were on alert. At the first sight of shadowy figures in the blinding snow, a cannon was fired. Montgomery was one of the first to die. Many of his officers died beside him. The soldiers panicked and fell back.

On the other side of the fortress, Benedict fared no better. He was hit in the leg. For a time, he leaned against a wall shouting orders, but he became so weak he had to be helped to the rear. Then there was no leadership for either attacking party. The Americans had to **concede** defeat. In the end, 426 Americans were captured and at least 60 killed. Of the British, 5 were killed and 13 wounded.

In a captured Catholic hospital outside the city, Benedict lay waiting for his leg to heal. Later the troops pulled back to Montreal. There Benedict learned that the Continental Congress had made him a brigadier general. He hoped he would have another chance to attack Quebec, but when spring arrived, he still had no reinforcements. His remaining men were weak with hunger and disease. In May a British fleet of 15 ships came up the St. Lawrence River full of enemy reinforcements. The Americans could stay no longer.

When the retreat finally occurred, Benedict's men were the last to leave. After loading his men on waiting boats, Benedict took the saddle off his horse and turned and shot the animal in the head, thus preventing the enemy from using it. As he sailed away from Canada, he began to think about the importance of Lake Champlain. What the Americans needed was

In the battle of Montreal, at least 60 American fighting men were killed, including General Montgomery (pictured here).

a strong fleet of ships to protect the important lake from advancing British troops. Surely he could do something about that.

Under Benedict's supervision, shipbuilders such as these constructed a fleet of 16 warships on Lake Champlain. Benedict was a good leader and inspired the sailors he trained.

4

Arnold's Brave Fleet

The retreating Americans went all the way back to Crown Point, at the southern end of Lake Champlain. While their regiments were still high in number, they were terribly low in morale. As John Adams reported to the Continental Congress, "Our army at Crown Point is an object of wretchedness to fill a humane mind with horror . . . no clothes, beds, blankets, no medicines; no **victuals**, but salt pork and flour."

Meanwhile, the British at the St. Lawrence River were transporting their ships overland in sections to be reassembled on the lake. They had well-armed ships under the command and direction of the Royal Navy. The Americans had only four small vessels with a total of 36 guns. General Gates ordered Benedict to supervise the construction of as many new warships as he could put together. Overjoyed, Benedict leaped at the chance.

Benedict gathered craftsmen to build the boats; then he trained men to operate them. Many of the recruits had never been on a ship before. Benedict always performed best when the odds were stacked against him. His confidence cheered the men, and they worked well under his leadership. By the end of August his fleet of 16 vessels sailed northward to meet the British.

On October 11, when lookouts spotted the British warships, Benedict situated his fleet in a channel between Valcour Island and the mainland. His planned surprise attack failed when they were spotted by the British in advance. But the wind was against the British. Only 17 of

During the battle of Valcour Island, the huge British cannons ripped apart the smaller American boats. The smoke and noise from the guns made ships' battles a terrifying experience.

the enemy's gunboats were able to maneuver into the narrow channel. During the raging battle, Benedict ran around the bloody deck helping the gunners to make good aim, all the time shouting orders and encouraging his men to keep up the fight. The huge and power-ful guns of the British ships were ripping the smaller American boats to shreds.

When nightfall came, the British formed a line between the tip of the island and the main-land. In the morning they would close in for the final kill. But Benedict would never surrender. Under a cover of dense fog, he ordered his fleet to slip past the enemy line. No one was to speak, no lights were to be lit. As soon as they were out of range, they rowed as fast as they could toward Fort Ticonderoga.

The British caught up with the slower ships and captured them, but Benedict was able to beach the faster boats. He ordered all of his ships that had eluded the British to be burned to keep them from falling into enemy hands. General Benedict Arnold and his remaining 100 men then set out on the long walk to the fort. The British, thinking it was too late in the season for a full-scale offensive, withdrew to Canada to await the spring. Many Americans would later say that it was certainly Benedict's brave fight that delayed the invasion by the British from the north.

For his extremely brave actions, Benedict fully expected to be hailed as a hero and given proper recognition. The Congress did not see things that way. When Benedict learned that five other officers had been promoted to Major General, and all were his juniors, he was embittered beyond words. He felt that the Congress had a personal grudge against him. The truth was that promotions were often decided to balance the number of senior officers from each state. Connecticut already had filled its quota of two major generals.

General Washington accepted this method of running the war, but Benedict did not. He demanded a court of inquiry. Washington tried to calm Benedict by giving him command of the Hudson Highlands. Benedict was not interested. He said he was going to Philadelphia to turn in his resignation. By April, however, he still had not gone to Philadelphia. He was at home in New Haven, brooding. His problems were not totally military. A young Tory girl whom he had courted in Boston decided to marry a civilian—a druggist. Again Benedict's ego was badly bruised.

Early one morning Benedict was roused from bed by General David Wooster, who told him that the British were on the move and they were marching to Danbury. The two Patriots rode hard and fast, gathering militia as they went, but it was too late. When they arrived, Danbury was in flames. Benedict and Wooster quickly agreed on a plan to retaliate by attacking the British while they were on their way back from Danbury.

During the fierce fighting that followed, in which the Patriots were greatly outnumbered, Benedict's horse was shot. As the horse fell over, Benedict could not leap free. Pinned beneath the horse, he found himself face to face with a Tory bayonet. In a lightning-swift

In one battle Benedict's horse was shot, but he urged his men to keep on fighting. Because of his bravery, he was promoted and he received a new horse.

move, the disabled Benedict whipped out his pistol and killed the Tory instantly. Somehow he found another horse and tried to gather his scattered men. He begged them to keep on fighting, reminding them of the freedom to be gained. But when they saw the British troops coming from Norwalk, it was no use. They were done fighting for the day.

The destruction in Danbury was great—ammunition, food, and supplies had all been lost in the fire. But Benedict was at last a hero. The Congress made him a major general and voted to give him a horse for his gallant conduct. Washington even wrote a commendation saying that Benedict was a brave officer. The promotion still did not suit Benedict because he was still at the bottom of the list. Four other major generals were his superiors.

Benedict was also having problems getting reimbursements from the Congress. He demanded repayment for expenses, but he had no receipts to present for the purchases. He seemed to think if he presented a figure, the Congress should pay him without question. If Congress wanted detailed records, he contended, they should have supplied him a **paymaster**. Some of the receipts for Benedict's purchases were lost in the chaos in Canada. Two centuries later, captured ledgers were found in a Quebec library.

More than the money, Benedict was concerned about his honor. To be questioned about his honesty meant his honor was in question. He could not stand this kind of insult. He was again ready to resign. Benedict's determination lasted until he heard that Ticonderoga had fallen back into enemy hands, and that British General John Burgoyne and his forces were moving rapidly down from Canada toward Albany. Benedict was off at once to help with the northern army.

In the staging area near Saratoga, New York, Benedict came under the leadership of General Horatio Gates. The two men were total opposites—Gates was cautious and careful; Benedict was headstrong and reckless. Gates held a strong position high on a bluff overlooking the Hudson River. He had several brigades spread out from there in strategic positions. Gates's plan was to wait for an attack. After all, he knew that the British were low on supplies from their long march from Canada. Benedict disagreed, urging Gates to attack Burgoyne during his approach.

Gates did not trust Benedict, and he did not agree with his tactics. When the battle began, there was no holding Benedict back. Disobeying orders, he jumped on a strong horse, and yelling to the nearest soldiers to follow, he led an attack. As he had done before, Benedict ignored danger and rode into the hail of bullets. "Come on boys!" he shouted to his men.

Urging his men forward, he boldly led them to assault the enemy behind their **breastworks,** yelling encouragement to his men all the way. In the fierce fighting, Benedict was shot in the leg–the same leg that had been wounded in the battle at Montreal.

The battle with Burgoyne was over, and thanks to Benedict's leadership, the Americans had made the entire British position helpless. The British had lost another 600 men, and now Burgoyne was on the retreat. In a matter of days, Burgoyne, the British officer who had once

Benedict bravely led an attack at Saratoga, New York. Over 600 British soldiers were killed. Here British General Burgoyne surrenders to General Gates.

made fun of the Patriots, was ready to surrender. On October 16, General John Burgoyne handed his sword to General Gates instead of Benedict.

For Benedict it was a bittersweet victory. He was so miserable that he stated he wished the bullet had struck his heart instead of his leg.

A street in colonial Philadelphia, where Benedict was assigned as military governor. He not only acted like a dictator but also made money by selling goods he had seized from the citizens.

Philadelphia and Peggy Shippen

or three months Benedict lay in an Albany hospital. Only his furious anger kept the surgeons from removing his leg. As he lay there recuperating he was riddled with discouragement and doubts. Would he be crippled the rest of his life? Were his fighting days over? At last he was sent home. His leg was in a massive cast called a "fracture box." New Haven gave the general a hero's welcome, and a grateful General Washington sent him **epaulets** and a sword knot.

Because of Benedict's disobedience, Gates had stripped him of his rank. But there was so much pressure on the Continental Congress to give Benedict a reward that his rank was eventually restored. Washington wrote requesting that Benedict come to Valley Forge to discuss his next assignment. When Washington saw the extent of Benedict's injury, however, he decided to install Benedict as the military governor over Philadelphia. At the camp in Valley Forge, Benedict signed the oath of **allegiance,** which was by then required of all officers.

The British had occupied the capital city Philadelphia for nine months under the leadership of General William Howe. Howe was so comfortable in Philadelphia that he passed the time by entertaining Loyalist ladies with costume balls, concerts, and plays. One would hardly have guessed there was a war going on nearby. But when the French actively entered into the war, things changed and the British evacuated Philadelphia. In June 1778 Benedict marched into the city while bells rang, guns boomed, and people cheered. But they did not cheer for long.

Benedict quickly ordered military law and took possession of shops and supplies. Very soon he was despised as a dictator. The citizens of Philadelphia would have disliked him even more if they had known he was misusing his power to take money for himself. Benedict was selling the goods he took for a hefty profit. He moved into the elegant John Penn House and drove around town in a coach with four horses. The feeling of power and prestige that he had always longed for was finally his. He had more than one reason to increase his personal fortune. He had met a beautiful 16-year-old girl named Peggy Shippen and was determined to court and marry her.

Peggy was the daughter of a Quaker, Judge Edward Shippen. Judge Shippen had tried his best to remain neutral throughout the war and, as a result, became poorer and poorer. Peggy was the youngest of five children and extremely spoiled. While the British occupied the city she was in the center of the social whirl. British officers, such as the talented and handsome Major John André, paid attention to her and flirted with her.

The arrival of the Americans seemed to spell the end to Peggy Shippen's good times. But then she met Benedict. Once again she was the belle of the balls held at the Penn Mansion. When Benedict first proposed marriage to Peggy, her father refused, but he later gave in. The two were engaged early in 1779 and planned a spring wedding. Benedict meanwhile sent for his sister, Hannah, and proceeded to purchase a mansion for his new bride. He needed money, but where would he get it? A new idea hatched in his head—to be put in charge of a fleet of **privateers**. When Congress heard the offer, they turned it down flat.

Benedict was never one to act in a diplomatic manner. Instead he usually persuaded and manipulated, offending many people and making many enemies. While he was busy

Peggy Shippen was from a prominent Philadelphia family. She became Benedict's second wife at the age of 17.

looking out for himself in Philadelphia, others were beginning to suspect his wrong dealings. Joseph Reed, a man who despised Benedict, headed up the governing body for the state of Pennsylvania. Reed was determined to remove Benedict from his position. He and the other members of the council printed a proclamation listing a number of accusations of wrongs committed by Benedict. The proclamation was sent to state governments, to the Congress, and was printed in some newspapers.

Benedict was furious and demanded a court martial proceeding to clear his name. The Pennsylvania council wanted him tried in a civilian court. As the arguments raged back and forth, Benedict felt he had had all the political suspicions and accusations he could handle. He resigned from his position.

On April 8, 1779, Benedict and his beloved Peggy Shippen were married in a small private ceremony in the home of Judge Shippen.

Benedict's future at this time was terribly uncertain. There would be no more gallant rides into battle because of his injury. He had not been paid in months, and money was losing its value. And now, because his name had not been cleared, Benedict was forced to sit and wait. The court martial was delayed several times.

Benedict's resentment against the Americans continued to fester, and Peggy fed into this resentment. They both agreed that the war was dragging on and accomplishing nothing. Peggy could not understand why the Americans did not just agree to Britain's terms and give up. She could see no importance in the quest for independence.

Assorted rumors floated about that the British were looking for American officers who would change sides. Benedict heard these rumors and considered the options. If he could not win the war for the Americans, perhaps he could be the one to bring the war to an end. He was sure that hundreds of weary Americans would follow him to the other side. He was also sure that his services would be worth a great deal of money to the British.

British General Henry Clinton, to whom Benedict offered his services in an effort to help end the war. The British did want Benedict's help—as a spy.

Peggy knew just the right person to contact to make such a deal—her old friend and admirer, John André. At the time André was an aide to

General Henry Clinton and in charge of all British intelligence in America. Peggy even knew a man who was a go-between—the local merchant, Joseph Stansbury. Stansbury was sympathetic to the British and traveled freely from Pennsylvania to New York on regular business trips.

Satisfied that the man was trustworthy, Benedict and Peggy gave Stansbury a message that Benedict was offering his services to Clinton. Benedict was pleased with what he had done. He thought he might just become a hero again after all.

West Point, New York, is located on the Hudson River. Benedict was put in command of the important military fort there. He secretly planned to give the fort over to the British.

Turncoat

pon receiving Benedict's message, André immediately took it to Clinton. At first neither believed that it was actually from Benedict. Clinton advised André to proceed slowly and carefully, and to promise little.

Benedict was shocked when he received the reply. What the British wanted was for Benedict to pretend to remain a Patriot, take leadership of a large military base, and then turn it over to the enemy. They ignored his offer to come to their side as a leader. What they wanted was a spy.

So the bargaining began. Plans were complicated

and dangerous. The British required that an intricate secret code be used, which took long hours to write out. The British held out for Benedict to take a command, and Benedict held out until he knew how much money they would pay him. All of this took many months.

Benedict's long-awaited court martial took place in December 1779. Because of his ability to lie in a convincing manner, only two counts were brought against him. These resulted in his being given only a **reprimand** from General Washington. But even this outcome upset Benedict. He might have done wrong, but he didn't want to be blamed. Soon after the court martial had ended, the treasury board found Benedict's records to be in a scramble. As near as they could calculate, Benedict owed the government nearly $2,000.

The spring of 1780 was dismal for the entire country. The British had made huge advances into the South, taking Savannah and Charleston. Benedict saw this as the end of the fight for freedom. He began to think of a command post that could be given over to the British. West Point seemed to be the perfect answer. Quietly he sold his property and transferred his funds to London. Making a visit to West Point, he studied the layout and fed information to the British. He did this before he had received command of the fort.

Eventually Benedict did receive command of West Point, simply because he asked Washington for it, and Washington trusted him. By August 5, Benedict was living in the former home of a Tory, Beverly Robinson. The home was situated across the Hudson River from West Point. On August 24, he received a letter from André promising 20,000 pounds for turning over the fort. Things were turning out better than he ever expected. He sent for Peggy and their newborn son, Edward, to come and join him.

John André, home from fighting in the South, was now a general. He was excited about the possibility of having West Point delivered into

A self-portrait of John André, a British general who plotted with Benedict. André was captured by Americans and executed as a spy.

British hands. He too had visions of being hailed as a conquering hero.

General Clinton, meanwhile, warned André not to go behind American lines and not to assume a disguise. He also forbade André to carry any papers with him in case he was caught. If taken while in uniform, he would be considered a prisoner and not a spy. Prisoners were exchanged, but spies were hanged.

Clinton and André thought of a simple plot that could be carried out in daylight. The plan involved the owner of the house, Mr. Robinson. But these and several other plans went very wrong. It seemed the meeting between André and Benedict might never take place.

When at last André was brought ashore from the British ship *Vulture* on September 20, he and Benedict met at night in the nearby woods. Benedict gave André copies of a map of the West Point defenses. They talked until dawn of the strategy for taking the fort. Since there was no chance André could return to the boat without being seen, Benedict took him behind American lines to the home of a man named Joshua Smith. In the meantime an American shore battery began firing on the *Vulture,* causing the ship to head downstream for safety. This meant André would have to travel a great distance to return to his ship.

Matters were becoming more complicated.

Benedict insisted André change into civilian clothes, after which he folded the papers and put them in André's stockings. He wrote out passes so André could make it safely back through the American lines. Benedict felt secure and confident as André left. Soon he would be a very rich man.

On September 25, Benedict was shocked to receive a letter saying that a man named John Anderson (André's code name) had been captured. The suspicious papers that were found in the prisoner's stockings had been sent at once to General Washington. In a panic Benedict ran upstairs to tell Peggy everything had been discovered. Because General Washington was on his way, Benedict's panic was multiplied. He jumped on his horse, tore down a steep ravine, and headed for his private barge. He ordered the bargemen to head for Stony Point. He directed them to sail out to where the *Vulture* was anchored, insisting he had official business with the captain.

The officers in charge of the *Vulture* expected that it was André returning from his mission and not Benedict. Benedict thought the British soldiers should be overjoyed to get his services, but when they learned André had been captured, they were angered instead. To prove his worth to the British officers, Benedict approached the unsuspecting bargemen, offering to make each of them non-commissioned officers if they deserted to the British cause. To his surprise, they all refused. In anger, Benedict had them thrown in the ship's brig as prisoners. (They were later released by General Clinton.)

André was tried on September 29, 1780, and

When Benedict fled from the Robinson house, Peggy went into hysterics. Those around her felt sure she was innocent of her husband's betrayal. Years later, when General Clinton's papers were examined, her part in the plot was revealed.

Peggy and Benedict eventually had four sons and a daughter. After Benedict died, Peggy sold her house and began to pay off all her husband's debts. She succeeded in doing so before she died in 1804.

hanged as a spy. This angered General Clinton, who had loved André as a son. It had been Benedict's idea for André to change clothes, and Benedict's idea for him to conceal the papers. For this reason Clinton would have little to do with Benedict. The other Tories in British-held New York, to which Benedict had deserted, felt much the same way. Benedict's dream of fame had been totally destroyed.

When Benedict later tried to tempt American soldiers to desert from the Continental Army, he was surprised that only about 60 men volunteered. He had fooled himself into thinking they would fall like dominoes. On the contrary, Benedict's act of treason had caused

General Clinton appealed to Washington to spare André's life, but Washington would not change his mind. André's final request was that he be shot as a soldier, not hanged as a spy. The request was denied. The American officers who attended him during his last days came to respect him. André went to the gallows cheerfully, wearing his uniform that he'd sent for. His last words were, "I would have you gentlemen bear me witness that I die like a brave man."

the Americans to draw together even more tightly.

The British became the losers in a bad bargain. What they wanted was West Point; what they got was an arrogant American general who was hated by all Americans. Clinton finally used Benedict in raids in Virginia and New London, a town 12 miles from Benedict's hometown of Norwich. The destruction from these surprise raids was widespread, but Benedict took no joy in them. He could no longer rush headlong into battle because there were people who wanted to kill him. He slept with two pistols by his side.

On October 19, 1781, British General Cornwallis surrendered at Yorktown, and the war officially ended. In January 1782 Benedict and his family boarded a ship and sailed for Britain. There he was befriended by the king and queen and was seen often at the palace.

Soon, though, the power in Britain shifted and the **Whigs** ousted the Tories, after which

Benedict and his family were no longer popular.

Benedict was given a lifetime pension of 500 pounds a year, which is far more than any American officer made. Had it been used wisely, the family could have lived on it comfortably. But Benedict was a slave to his lavish lifestyle. For a time, he turned to trading in the West Indies, but he was constantly in debt and always involved in one scrap after another. He died in June 1801 at age 60, a disappointed, bitter man.

Benedict had been a fearless leader and a brilliant battlefield general. Sadly, in the end, his entire life proved to be a waste of talents and abilities.

In Saratoga, New York, a monument recognizes Benedict's contribution to the victory won there. There is no name on the monument.

GLOSSARY

aggression–hostile action or behavior

allegiance–loyalty to one's country, government, or ruler

apothecary–a person who is trained in the preparation of drugs and medicines; pharmacist

apprentice–a person learning a trade from a skilled worker

bateaux–flat-bottomed boats with flaring sides

breastworks–quickly-constructed fortifications, usually about breast-high

concede–to admit as true or real

cooper–a person who makes wooden barrels or casks

epaulets–a shoulder ornament on certain military dress uniforms

militia–a group of civilian men called into the military only during emergencies

Patriot–a person who believed America should be a country separate from Britain

paymaster–a person in charge of paying wages or salaries

powder house–a building where gunpowder and ammunition were stored

privateers–armed private ships that are allowed to attack enemy ships

reprimand–a statement of severe or formal disapproval

Tory–during the Revolutionary War, a colonist who sided with England; in England, a member of a political party opposed to the Whigs

valet–a male attendant who cares for a gentleman's clothing and performs personal services

victuals–food supplies

Whig–during the Revolutionary War, a colonist who supported the war against Britain; in Britain, a member of a political party opposed to the Tories

CHRONOLOGY

1741   Born Benedict Arnold on January 14 in Norwich, Connecticut.

1755   Is apprenticed to the Lathrop brothers in New Haven.

1757   Joins local militia to fight the French and Indian War.

1762   Finishes apprenticeship; opens a store in New Haven.

1765   Starts shipping business; becomes captain of his own ship.

1767   Marries first wife, Margaret (Peggy) Mansfield.

1774   Joins the New Haven militia called the Footguards.

1775   Promoted to the rank of colonel; helps to capture Fort Ticonderoga along with Ethan Allen; first wife dies; leads forces through Maine wilderness to join forces with Montgomery in the attack against Quebec; is wounded; promoted to brigadier general.

1776   Creates a makeshift navy fleet on Lake Champlain; fights a British fleet that is forced to retreat; fights in battle at Danbury and leg is injured; promoted to major general.

1777   Leads the battle at Saratoga; is shot in the leg; British General Burgoyne surrenders to American General Gates at Saratoga.

1778   Signs the oath of allegiance at Valley Forge; takes command of Philadelphia.

1779   Marries Peggy Shippen; his court martial takes place; begins secret negotiations with the British.

1780 Takes command of West Point; meets with British General John André; André is captured and hanged as a spy.

1781 British Commander Cornwallis surrenders at Yorktown; the Revolutionary War is over.

1782 Sails with family to Britain.

1801 Dies in London.

REVOLUTIONARY WAR TIME LINE ═══

1765   The Stamp Act is passed by the British. Violent protests against it break out in the colonies.

1766   Britain ends the Stamp Act.

1767   Britain passes a law that taxes glass, painter's lead, paper, and tea in the colonies.

1770   Five colonists are killed by British soldiers in the Boston Massacre.

1773   People are angry about the taxes on tea. They throw boxes of tea from ships in Boston harbor into the water. It ruins the tea. The event is called the Boston Tea Party.

1774   The British pass laws to punish Boston for the Boston Tea Party. They close Boston harbor. Leaders in the colonies meet to plan a response to these actions.

1775   The battles of Lexington and Concord begin the American Revolution.

1776   The Declaration of Independence is signed. France and Spain give money to help the Americans fight Britain. Nathan Hale is captured by the British. He is charged with being a spy and is executed.

1777   Leaders choose a flag for America. The American troops win some important battles over the British. General Washington and his troops spend a very cold, hungry winter in Valley Forge.

1778 France sends ships to help the Americans win the war. The British are forced to leave Philadelphia.

1779 French ships head back to France. The French support the Americans in other ways.

1780 Americans discover that Benedict Arnold is a traitor. He escapes to the British. Major battles take place in North and South Carolina.

1781 The British surrender at Yorktown.

1783 A peace treaty is signed in France. British troops leave New York.

1787 The U.S. Constitution is written. Delaware becomes the first state in the Union.

1789 George Washington becomes the first president. John Adams is vice president.

FURTHER READING

Hughes, Libby. *Valley Forge.* New York: Dillon Press, 1993.

Lukes, Bonnie. *The American Revolution.* San Diego: Lucent Books, 1996.

Old, Wendie C. *George Washington.* Springfield, NJ: Enslow Publishers, 1997.

Peacock, Louise. *Crossing the Delaware: A History in Many Voices.* New York: Antheneum Books For Young Readers, 1998.

Seymour, Reit. *Guns for General Washington: A Story of the American Revolution.* San Diego: Harcourt Brace Jovanovich, 1990.

INDEX

PICTURE CREDITS ===

ABOUT THE AUTHOR ══════════

NORMA JEAN LUTZ, who lives in Tulsa, Oklahoma, has been writing professionally since 1977. She is the author of more than 250 short stories and articles as well as 36 books—fiction and non-fiction. Of all the writing she does, she most enjoys writing children's books.

Senior Consulting Editor **ARTHUR M. SCHLESINGER, JR.** is the leading American historian of our time. He won the Pulitzer Prize for his book *The Age of Jackson* (1945), and again for *A Thousand Days* (1965). This chronicle of the Kennedy Administration also won a National Book Award. He has written many other books, including a multi-volume series, *The Age of Roosevelt.* Professor Schlesinger is the Albert Schweitzer Professor of the Humanities at the City University of New York, and has been involved in several other Chelsea House projects, including the Colonial Leaders series of biographies on the most prominent figures of early American history.